The Girl Who Caught The Stars

Anila Asif

Published by Anila Asif, 2024.

THE GIRL WHO CAUGHT THE STARS

First edition. December 24, 2024.

ISBN: 979-8227349552

Written by Anila Asif.

The Girl Who Caught the Stars

Chapter 1: The Secret of Riverstone Creek

Lily Bennett had always felt a special connection to Riverstone Creek. Her family had been visiting the peaceful, winding creek for generations, passing down the tradition of fishing and enjoying the serene beauty of the place. Every day after school and on weekends, Lily would make her way to the creek with her trusty fishing rod, eager to spend hours

lost in the calming rhythm of casting her line and watching the water ripple beneath her. One warm afternoon, while casting her line near an old, moss-covered stone bridge that had been standing for as long as anyone could remember, Lily noticed something unusual. Beneath the water's surface, partially hidden among the tangled roots of an ancient willow tree, lay a weathered piece of parchment.

Curiosity piqued, she knelt down, carefully reaching into the cool water to retrieve it. The map, though tattered and faded with age, still held some shape. It depicted the creek and the surrounding forest, but something about it was different—there were markings she had never seen before, pointing to a hidden spot deep in the woods. Along with the map was a cryptic note, written in elegant but fading handwriting:

"Find the fish that lives beneath the stars, and your wish will be granted. The river holds secrets that only the brave can see. Follow the map, and you will find what you seek."

Lily's heart raced. The mention of a fish that could grant wishes sounded like something out of a fairy tale, but the idea that it could be real intrigued her beyond measure. She knew that Riverstone Creek was special, but the idea that it might hold a legendary secret like this was beyond her wildest dreams.

She carefully tucked the map and note into her pocket, her mind racing with possibilities. Could the legend be true? Was there really a fish in the creek that could grant wishes? Lily had to find out.

The legend of the Starfin fish had always been a quiet whisper in the town, passed down as a half-forgotten story from old fishermen.

Most people dismissed it as myth, but Lily felt something deep inside her, a pull toward the adventure that awaited. Determined to uncover the truth, she decided she would follow the map.
As the sun began to set, casting an orange glow over the creek, Lily made her way home, her thoughts consumed by the mystery she had just uncovered.

Tomorrow, she would begin her journey to find the legendary fish, unaware of the adventures, challenges, and discoveries that would come her way. Little did she know, this journey would change her life in ways she never imagined.

Chapter 2: The River's Whisper

The next morning, Lily couldn't shake the excitement bubbling inside her. The map in her pocket felt heavier than ever, urging her to begin her quest. After breakfast, she grabbed her fishing gear and headed straight to the creek, determined to find the legendary Starfin fish. The water sparkled under the sun, the familiar sound of the creek flowing peacefully, as though nothing had changed.

But for Lily, everything was different now. The creek held a secret, one she was ready to uncover.

As she walked along the riverbank, her mind raced with thoughts of the Starfin—what would it look like? Was it really magical? Would it grant her wish? The possibilities seemed endless. But as she passed by her favorite fishing spot, she noticed someone sitting on an old wooden stool near the water, casting his line with slow, steady movements.

It was Mr. Finn, a local fisherman who had lived in the town for as long as anyone could remember. His gray beard and weathered face reflected a lifetime spent by the water. He was known for his wisdom, and many people in town came to him for advice on all things related to the creek.

“Morning, Lily,” Mr. Finn said, his voice soft yet firm, as though he’d been expecting her. “You’re up early today.”

Lily smiled, but she couldn't contain her excitement. "I'm going fishing," she said, her voice almost a whisper, as if she were sharing a secret. "I found something... a map. It's supposed to lead me to the Starfin fish. The one that grants wishes."
Mr. Finn raised an eyebrow, then slowly took a deep breath. "Ah, the Starfin... I've heard the legend many times.

You're not the first to be drawn to it, Lily." He paused,

looking at her with a knowing expression. "But there's more to the story than what the map tells you."

Lily's heart skipped a beat. "What do you mean?" she asked, sitting down next to him on the bank.

Mr. Finn leaned back, his gaze drifting to the flowing water. "The river doesn't give up its secrets easily," he said. "It's patient, and it expects the same from those who seek its gifts. Many have come before you, eager to find the Starfin, but few truly understand what they're asking for. The river is not just a body of water—it's alive, with its own voice. You've got to listen carefully to hear it."

Lily looked at the creek, her brow furrowing in confusion. "Listen to it? How?"

"Ah, that's the trick," Mr. Finn replied with a slow smile. "You've got to quiet your mind. The river speaks in whispers, in the rustling of the leaves, the ripple of the water.

It tells you more than you think—about the weather, about where the fish are, about the way the land moves beneath the surface. If you listen, it will guide you. But if you rush ahead, chasing only the wish, you might miss the real magic that's already here."

Lily sat in silence for a moment, reflecting on his words. She had always loved the creek, but she had never truly listened to it before. She had simply cast her line, waiting for a bite, eager for the thrill of the catch. But what if there was more to it? What if the river had secrets it wanted to share, if only she took the time to understand?

Mr. Finn turned to her, his old eyes twinkling. “The Starfin may grant a wish, but it’s not the only treasure the creek holds. The river has its own rhythm, and sometimes the greatest rewards come from simply being in tune with it.”

Lily nodded, a sense of calm washing over her. She didn't know if she would find the Starfin, but she now understood that her journey wasn't just about catching a mythical fish. It was about connecting with the river, respecting its mysteries, and learning from its quiet wisdom.

"I'll listen," Lily said softly, her voice filled with a new resolve. "I'll learn what the river wants to teach me."

Mr. Finn smiled, pleased with her response.

"Good girl. Take your time, and let the river be your guide."

With those words, Lily stood up, her heart full of anticipation. She took a deep breath, closed her eyes for a moment, and listened. The sound of the creek was gentle, but it was there—soft whispers, like the river was speaking to her, telling her to slow down and pay attention. It was then that she realized: the river's secrets weren't just about the fish—it was about everything around her, everything that had always been there.

As Lily moved forward, the world around her felt different. She could sense the beauty of the water, the energy of the trees, and the life of the forest in a way she never had before. And with that newfound awareness, she knew her adventure had just begun. The Starfin was still out there, but now she understood that the true magic of her journey was in discovering the river itself.

Chapter 3: A New Friend in the Water

Lily was up early the next morning, eager to continue her search for the Starfin. She had spent hours the day before walking along the creek, listening to the water, trying to follow the clues she'd discovered. But despite her best efforts, she hadn't found any sign of the mythical fish. She was starting to feel like she was missing something, and the map in her pocket seemed more like a puzzle than a guide.

That's when she heard a voice behind her.
"Hey, you're fishing here too?"
Lily turned around to see a boy about her age standing near the water's edge, holding a fishing rod. His brown hair was tousled from the wind, and his wide grin showed a love for fishing that matched her own.
"Yeah, I guess so," Lily said, feeling a bit shy. "I'm Lily. And you are?"

"Jake," he replied with a wave, stepping closer. "I've seen you around. You're always out here, right?"

Lily nodded. "I live nearby. I've been fishing here for years."

Jake's eyes lit up. "Same here! I've been coming to Riverstone Creek with my dad ever since I can remember. But I've never fished anywhere other than the usual spots." He looked around, as though scanning the water for something.

"You seem like you know this place pretty well. Maybe you've got some good tips for me?"

Lily hesitated for a moment, then smiled. Maybe this would be the perfect chance to talk about her search for the Starfin. "Actually, I'm looking for something... a special fish," she began, keeping her voice low. "I found an old map, and it says there's a fish here that can grant wishes. It's called Starfin."

Jake raised an eyebrow, his interest piqued. "A fish that grants wishes? That sounds like something out of a legend."

"That's what I thought too," Lily said, pulling the map from her pocket and showing it to him. "But I think it's real. The map shows a hidden part of the creek, and I'm trying to find it."

Jake looked at the map for a moment, then grinned.

"That's awesome! I love a good adventure. Want some company? I could use a challenge."

Lily thought for a moment. She wasn't sure about teaming up with someone else—this journey felt so personal. But then again, Jake seemed genuinely passionate about fishing, and it could be useful to have someone else along. Besides, the creek wasn't an easy place to navigate alone.

"Alright, let's do it," Lily agreed, a spark of excitement in her voice. "But we've got to be careful. We don't know what we're dealing with."

Together, the two of them set off through the thick woods, following the map's winding path along the creek. The forest was lush and vibrant, filled with the sounds of birds and rustling leaves. As they walked, they shared stories about their lives, their favorite fishing spots, and what drew them to the creek in the first place. Lily was surprised to find that Jake shared her deep connection to the water. He didn't just fish for fun—he spoke of the creek with the same respect and wonder that Lily had always felt.

The day was filled with adventure. They fished in new, uncharted spots along the creek, navigating tricky paths and thick underbrush. Along the way, they faced unexpected challenges: a sudden rainstorm forced them to seek shelter under a large oak tree, and at one point, they had to climb over a fallen log that blocked their path.

But through it all, they worked together, laughing and supporting each other. As the sun began to set, they decided to set up camp for the night by the creek. They built a small fire and roasted marshmallows, the crackling flames casting a warm glow over their faces. Lily couldn't remember the last time she'd had so much fun, and she was starting to feel like she wasn't alone in this journey anymore.

That evening, after they finished eating, they sat by the water, the moon reflecting on the surface. The air was cool, and the sound of the creek was soothing. It was a peaceful moment, and Lily felt content just being there, surrounded by the natural beauty of the place she loved.

As she sat quietly, staring into the water, something unusual caught her eye. There, just beneath the surface, a soft glow seemed to ripple through the water, like a faint light was moving through the creek.

“Jake... did you see that?” Lily whispered, her voice barely audible.

Jake turned toward the water, squinting into the darkness. “What do you mean?”

“There’s something down there,” Lily said, her pulse quickening. “It’s glowing.”

They both leaned closer to the edge of the creek,

their eyes wide with curiosity. For a moment, the water was still, and then, just as Lily was beginning to doubt herself, the glow reappeared. It wasn't just any light—it was a soft, silvery shimmer, moving gracefully through the water like a fish gliding in the moonlight.

Lily's heart raced. Could it be? Was this the Starfin? Without thinking, she grabbed her fishing rod, her hands trembling with excitement. Jake was already pulling out his own rod, ready to fish,

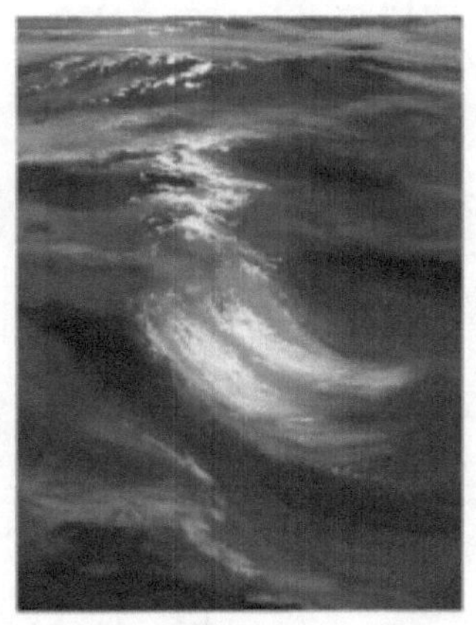

but Lily's mind was focused entirely on the glowing figure beneath the water.

For the first time in her life, the creek seemed alive with possibilities, and Lily knew that she was getting closer to her goal. The Starfin was real—and it was just beyond her reach.

"Let's try to catch it," she said, her voice steady with determination.

This time, it felt like the creek was on her side, whispering its secrets, guiding her toward the wish that awaited. Jake nodded, eager to help. Together, they cast their lines into the creek, their eyes fixed on the glowing figure beneath the surface, waiting for the moment when they would finally catch the fish that could change everything.

Chapter 4:
The Storm and the Lost Catch

The morning had been filled with excitement. Lily and Jake had been fishing for hours, following the map deeper into the woods, casting their lines into the creek with high hopes of finally catching the mythical Starfin. The glowing fish they had seen the night before lingered in their minds, like a beacon, guiding them closer to their goal.

But as the day wore on, the weather began to change. The wind picked up, rustling the trees and whipping the water into small waves. Dark clouds gathered on the horizon, blocking out the sun. By noon, the first drop of rain fell, followed quickly by another, then another, until the sky opened up, and a torrential downpour soaked everything in sight.

“We need to get out of here!” Jake shouted over the roar of the storm,

grabbing his gear as the rain poured down in sheets. Lily nodded, her heart pounding as the water around them began to rise. They had been fishing at the edge of the creek, and now the current was growing stronger by the minute. The creek, which had always been calm and gentle, was starting to swell with the rainwater, rushing faster and more violently than ever. The wind howled, bending trees and making it impossible to keep their footing.

Lily's fishing rod was pulled from her hands by a gust of wind, and Jake's tackle box tumbled into the water, floating away like a toy. The storm was fierce, and their gear was getting ruined by the minute.

"Jake, we have to go!" Lily shouted, her voice barely audible over the storm.

Jake nodded, his face grim as he scanned the creek for any signs of danger.

They quickly gathered their remaining belongings, but the water was rising too fast. The current was getting stronger, and they could feel the ground beneath them starting to shift, the creek becoming a rushing river. They had no choice but to abandon their mission for now.

With one last glance at the stormy water, Lily and Jake made their way up the creek to higher ground, huddling under the protection of a large oak tree.

As the rain continued to pour down in torrents, they set up a small campfire, its warm glow flickering in the wet, cold night. The storm raged on, but the fire crackled cheerfully, offering a small comfort amidst the chaos. Lily sat beside the fire, pulling her wet jacket tighter around her shoulders. She stared into the flames, her mind wandering.

The Starfin—the magical fish she had been chasing for so long—seemed so distant now, its glow fading in the dark recesses of her thoughts. In the midst of the storm, with their gear ruined and their plans interrupted, she found herself questioning the obsession that had driven her for so long.

She had been so focused on the legend of the Starfin, on finding that one elusive fish and making a wish, that she had forgotten why she loved fishing in the first place. Fishing had always been about more than catching a big fish—it was about being still, about connecting with the water, and listening to the quiet moments that nature offered. It was about the joy of simply being outside, feeling the gentle tug on the line, and appreciating the peaceful solitude by the water's edge.

Lily realized, as she stared into the flickering firelight, that she had lost sight of all of that. The chase for the Starfin had consumed her, and she had forgotten how much joy she found in the simple act of fishing itself.

The quiet mornings on the creek, the rustling leaves, the call of the birds—these were the things that had drawn her to the water in the first place. Not the wish, not the fish, but the serenity of being one with the natural world.

“What do you think, Jake?” Lily asked, her voice quieter now, softer. “Do you ever think we get so caught up in the chase that we forget why we started in the first place?”

Jake looked up from the fire, his face thoughtful. “Yeah,” he said, nodding slowly. “Sometimes it’s easy to forget that fishing isn’t just about the catch. It’s about the quiet moments. The time with nature. I mean, look at us right now. We’ve had a crazy day, but here we are, sitting by the fire, safe and warm. It’s not a big catch, but it’s a good moment.”

Lily smiled, feeling a weight lift off her shoulders.

The Starfin was still out there, but for now, it didn't matter. She didn't need the mythical fish to feel complete. What she had was the river, the woods, and a friend who understood the joy of being by the water, whether or not there was a wish at the end of the line.

As the storm raged on, the fire flickered and crackled between them. Lily looked up at the sky, watching the rain pour down, but for the first time in days, she felt at peace.

She had been so focused on finding the fish that she had forgotten about the simple, quiet moments that made the journey worthwhile. And now, sitting beside the fire, with the creek roaring in the distance, Lily realized that the true magic wasn't in the Starfin—it was in the way the river whispered, in the way the world came alive when you were still enough to listen.

"I think I'm starting to understand," Lily said softly, more to herself than to Jake. "It's not about the fish. It's about the river."

Jake grinned, his eyes reflecting the firelight. "Exactly."

The storm may have taken their catch for the day, but it had given Lily something even more valuable—a reminder that the greatest treasures weren't always the ones you set out to find. Sometimes, the best moments were the ones that came quietly, in the spaces between the storms, in the moments when you stopped chasing and just listened.

Chapter 5: The Wish Beneath the Stars

The storm had passed, leaving behind a clear, quiet night. The air was fresh and cool, with a soft breeze rustling the trees and the creek flowing gently once more. Lily stood on the riverbank, the water reflecting the stars above like a mirror. The moonlight illuminated the trees and the hills in the distance, casting long shadows and painting the world in shades of silver.

It was peaceful now, and the creek, though wild after the storm, seemed to have returned to its usual rhythm. Lily had come to the creek that night not in search of the Starfin—but to simply be with it again, to appreciate the quiet beauty of the place she had come to love even more deeply since her adventure had begun. After the storm, after the moments by the fire with Jake, and after realizing what truly mattered,

Lily felt a sense of calm she hadn't known before. The Starfin wasn't just about the fish—it was about the creek, the world around her, and her connection to nature.

As she sat on a rock by the water's edge, her fishing rod resting beside her, Lily reflected on everything she'd learned. The Starfin had been a dream at first—an idea that would make her wish come true. But now, she understood something greater.

The real wish wasn't a personal one. It was a wish for the future, for the creatures that called the river home, and for the generations who would come after her.

Just as she was about to stand up and leave, a sudden shimmer in the water caught her eye.

Her heart skipped a beat as she watched, her breath catching in her throat. There, beneath the surface, was a fish unlike any she had ever seen before.

Its scales were like liquid silver, glowing faintly in the moonlight. Its fins shimmered with an ethereal blue light, the glow flowing through the water like the stars in the sky. It was the Starfin—real, and more beautiful than she could have ever imagined. Lily stood frozen, her mind racing. She had heard the legend, seen the glow the night before, but seeing the Starfin in person felt surreal.

It moved gracefully through the water, its glowing fins leaving a trail of light behind it. Lily could hardly believe her eyes. The fish wasn't just a myth—it was a living, breathing miracle.

But as she watched it swim, Lily felt something stir inside her. She had been so focused on the idea of catching it, of making a wish, but now that she saw it—now that she understood the magic of the river, the true beauty of the creek and its creatures—she realized that her wish had already been granted. She had found something far more precious than a wish: she had found a world worth protecting.

The Starfin swam closer, as if it knew she was there, as if it had been waiting for this moment. Its eyes met hers, and Lily felt a deep connection, a sense of knowing that passed between them. She didn't need to make a wish for herself. She didn't need anything more.

In that moment, Lily understood that the greatest gift she could ask for wasn't for herself—it was for the creek, for the fish, and for the world that had given her so much. The Starfin was a symbol, a reminder of the wild beauty that needed to be protected. The river, the forest, the animals—it all depended on care, respect, and understanding. And Lily knew now that her true wish was to preserve the magic of the natural world, so future generations could experience it just as she had.

With a deep breath, Lily slowly stood up, her heart calm and full. She reached down to her fishing rod, but instead of casting her line into the water, she let it rest on the ground beside her. The Starfin was here, in its natural home, and that was where it belonged.

The fish swam closer, its glowing fins lighting up the water, casting ripples across the creek. For a moment, it seemed to pause, as if acknowledging Lily's decision.

Then, with a final flash of light, it darted back into the deeper waters, disappearing from view.

Lily smiled, feeling a profound peace settle in her heart. She didn't need to make a wish. She had already made the best decision she could. The creek, with its shimmering waters, its wild creatures, and its ancient secrets, would always be a part of her. And she would do everything in her power to protect it, to ensure that others could come here and experience the same magic she had found. As she stood on the bank, the stars twinkling above her and the creek flowing peacefully at her feet, Lily realized that this was the true gift—the beauty of the world, the connection to nature, and the knowledge that, sometimes, the greatest wish is the one that leads you to protect and cherish what you love.

The Starfin was gone, but the magic of the river would never fade. And Lily knew that, no matter where life took her, she would always carry that magic with her. The true wish, she thought, wasn't in a fish at all—it was in the love we give to the world around us.

www.ingramcontent.com/pod-product-compliance
Lightning Source LLC
LaVergne TN
LVHW040954150826
845672LV00002B/698

* 9 7 9 8 2 2 7 3 4 9 5 5 2 *